TRAVIS PASTRANA

DISCOVER THE LIFE OF A SPORTS STAR II

David and Patricia Armentrout

Rourke
Publishing LLC
Vero Beach, Florida 32964

www.rourkepublishing.com

PHOTO CREDITS: All photos © Steve Bruhn

Title page: *Travis Pastrana got his start in motocross competition.*

Editor: Frank Sloan

Cover and interior design by Nicola Stratford

Library of Congress Cataloging-in-Publication Data

Armentrout, David, 1962-
  Travis Pastrana / David and Patricia Armentrout.
     p. cm. — (Discover the life of a sports star II)
  Includes bibliographical references and index.
   ISBN 1-59515-133-8 (hardcover)
  1. Pastrana, Travis, 1983---Juvenile literature. 2. Motorcyclists--United States--Biography--Juvenile literature. 3. Motocross--United States--Juvenile literature. I. Armentrout, Patricia, 1960- II. Title. II. Series: Armentrout, David, 1962-   Discover the life of a sports star II.
   GV1060.2.P39A76 2004
   796.7'5'092--dc22

                                                    2004007641

Printed in the USA

CG/CG

Table of Contents

Travis takes home the gold at the 2002 Gravity Games after performing the back flip.

Travis Pastrana

Few athletes ever reach the highest level of their sport. For most, becoming a superstar is just a dream. Travis Pastrana's dream came true at a very young age. By age 14, Travis was a **motocross** superstar.

Born: October 8, 1983 in
  Annapolis, Maryland
Residence: Annapolis,
  Maryland
Best Event: Freestyle
Favorite Tricks: No-footer, Backflip

A Work in Progress

Most athletes work for years to master their sport. Travis Pastrana is no exception. Even though Travis is still a young man, he has over 15 years of riding experience. His parents gave him a small Honda Z-50 motorbike for Christmas when he was just four years old. It may be the best gift he ever received. Since then Travis has never looked back.

Motocross enthusiasts begin learning their sport at a very young age.

Accepting awards for a job well done is just part of the game.

Motocross Superstar

The word motocross is a combination of the words motorcycle and cross country. Motocross riders compete in different events on natural terrain outdoor tracks.

Supercross is a form of motocross that takes place on indoor tracks. Supercross tracks are usually shorter with steep, man-made hills and lots of obstacles. Travis competes in both motocross and supercross events.

Travis rides at a supercross competition.

Travis performs the "Superman Seat Grab" at the 2003 Gravity Games.

Freestyle

Travis's best event is the **freestyle** competition. In freestyle competition, riders get huge air and pull off monster tricks. Travis became the youngest World Freestyle Motocross Champion when he was 14.

Travis wins because he is a good rider and brings a fresh style to every competition. He invented or improved many of the best tricks in the sport.

Travis attempts a back flip in freestyle competition.

A World-Class Athlete

Travis has dominated freestyle competition most of his career. He is also a top competitor in other motocross events. He has won numerous national and international titles at both the **amateur** and **professional** levels.

Travis has also gained worldwide attention winning multiple gold medals in both the X Games and the Gravity Games. One thing everyone seems to agree on is that Travis Pastrana has brought excitement to the sport of motocross.

A Popular Spectator Sport

Motocross has become a popular spectator sport. **Sponsors**, hoping to draw attention to their products, sign the best riders to rich contracts. Travis signed with American Suzuki when he was only eight years old after winning his first amateur championship.

Money earned from competitions, videos, video games, sponsorships, and even "Travis" action figures, has made Travis a wealthy man.

Motocross events are held on dirt tracks all over the country.

A New House

Travis admits he enjoys the money he earns. Recently, he bought a new house. When the house was being built, Travis had two requests. First, he wanted a firemen's pole. Second, he wanted a pool built close enough to the house so that he could jump into it from the roof. Luckily, his parents talked him out of the second request. He did, however, have a motocross track built right in his own backyard.

Travis takes time to sign photos for young fans.

Travis goes down after bumping a fellow rider.

A Tough Sport

Motocross is a dangerous sport, even for superstars. Travis always takes safety seriously. Tricks are well planned, and he always wears safety gear, including a helmet and **body armor**. Even with safety precautions, riders do get hurt. Travis estimates he has broken more than 30 bones and has undergone surgery 12 times.

Planning for the Future

Travis understands there is more to life than riding a motorcycle. He hasn't let his success stand in the way of a good education. Travis worked hard and graduated from high school three years early. He began taking college courses when he was 15. Travis continues his studies at the University of Maryland. When his career as a competitor is over, Travis hopes to land a job in public relations or broadcasting.

Freestyle tricks leave spectators in awe.

The crowd cheers for Travis after competition.

Dates to Remember

1983	Born in Annapolis, Maryland
1992-1999	National Amateur Champion
1998	Wins World Freestyle Motocross Championship
1999	Gold Medalist at Summer Gravity Games
1999	Gold Medalist at X-Games
2000	Gold Medalist at Summer X-Games
2001	Gold Medalist at Summer X-Games
2002	Gold Medalist at Summer Gravity Games
2003	Missed most of the racing season due to injury
2004	Returns to racing in the AMA Supercross series

Glossary

amateur (AM uh tur) — someone who participates in a sport for pleasure rather than money

body armor (BOD ee AR mur) — protective gear worn by motocross riders

freestyle (FREE styl) — competitive event in which riders perform tricks

motocross (MOH tow kross) — a cross country motorcycle race

professional (pruh FESH un ul) — a paid instructor or athlete

sponsors (SPON surz) — companies or organizations that provide funding in exchange for advertising

supercross (SOO per kross) — a motocross event held at an indoor track or stadium

Index

Further Reading

Milan, Garth. Bales, Donny. *Freestyle Motocross: Jump Tricks from the Pros.* Motorbooks International, 2001

McGrath, Jeremy. *Wide Open: A Life in Supercross.* HarperEntertainment, 2004

Coombs, Davey. *MX: The Way of the Motocrosser.* Harry N. Abrams, 2003

Websites To Visit

www.expn.go.com/athletes/bios/PASTRANA_TRAVIS.html
www.motocross.com
www.gravitygames.com/athletes/

About The Authors

David and Patricia Armentrout have written many nonfiction books for young readers. They have had several books published for primary school reading. The Armentrouts live in Cincinnati, Ohio, with their two children.